How To Live On An Island

by Sandy Gingras

A CORMORANT BOOK

DOWN THE SHORE
P U B L I S H I N G

For information, address:
Down The Shore Publishing, Box 3100, Harvey Cedars, NJ 08008
Down The Shore and its logos are registered U.S. Trademarks.
Printed in Hong Kong on recycled paper. ♲ First printing, 1996.
10 9 8 7 6 5 4 3 2 1

Library of Congress Cataloging-in-Publication Data
    Gingras, Sandy, 1958-
        How to live on an island / by Sandy Gingras.
            p.   cm. -- (A cormorant book)
        ISBN 0-945582-32-3 (pbk.)
        1. Aphorisms and apothegms.   2. Islands--Quotations, maxims, etc.
    I. Title.   II. Series.
    PN6278.I68G56   1996
    741.5'973--dc20   95-19956
                                                     CIP

for morgAn

Every man, woman and child is an island (sorry John Donne, you're right too). We all know the feeling of crossing over water and understanding, with the sudden scent of a tide, what it is to come home to ourselves.

be Transported

fLOAT

make a splash

Listen in on shells

stretch

run with waves

Laugh Like a GULL

carry a bucket

BOOGie

Sugar yourself with sand

Ebb And flow

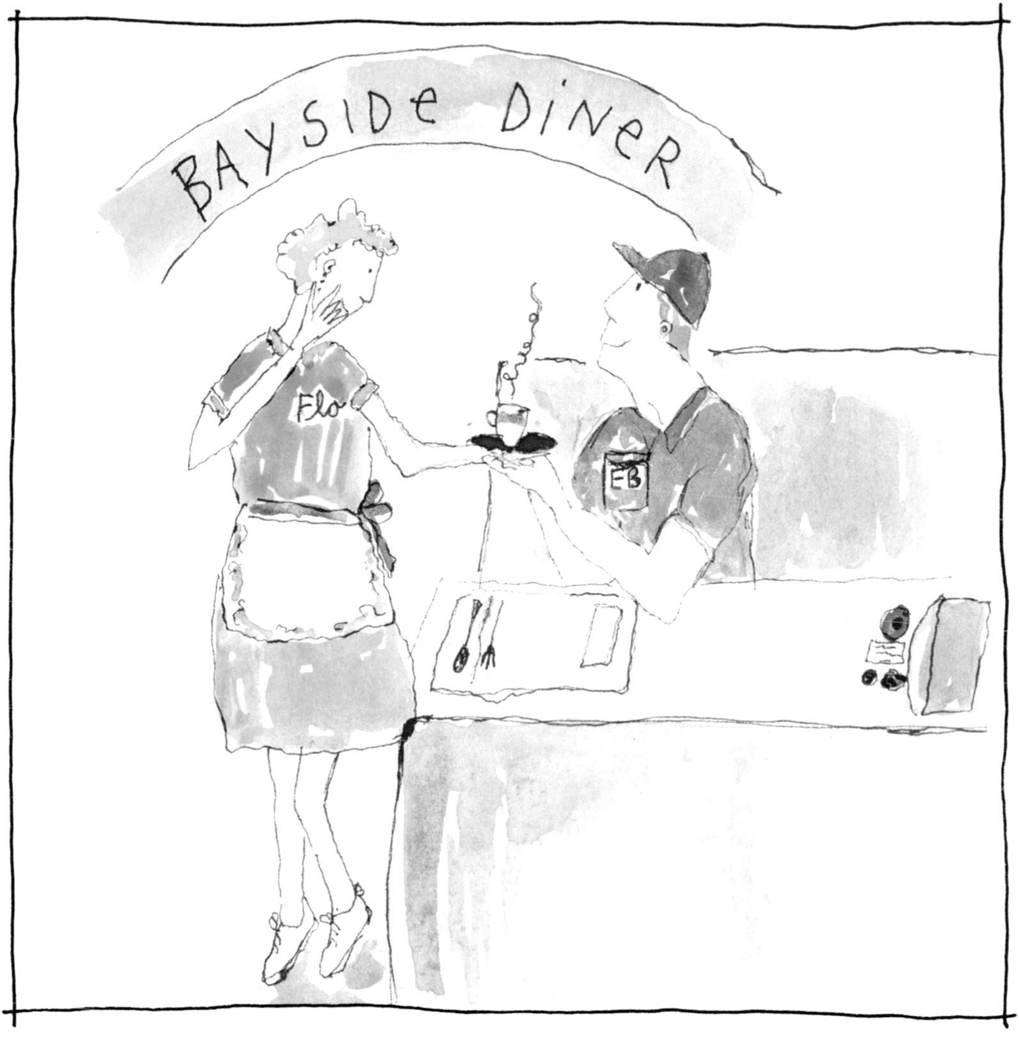
BAYSIDE DINER
Flo
EB

ride rusty bikes--
Go with the wind

CULTIVATE QUIET

Tune up your senses

WALK Tender

put Living things bACK

dANCE on edGeS

build CASTLes And LeAve
them for The moon
to find

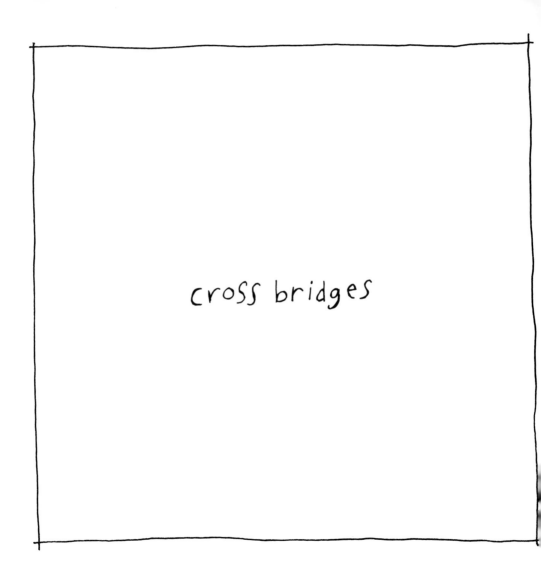

cross bridges

discover treasure

ThAnk

Down The Shore Publishing offers many other book and calendar titles (with a special emphasis on the mid-Atlantic coast). For a free catalog, or to be added to the mailing list, just send us a request:

Down The Shore Publishing
Box 3100, Harvey Cedars, NJ 08008.